THE FORGOTTEN FACTOR

RESOURCE CENTRE

Please return to:
Camp Qwanoes 250-246-3014

The Forgotten Factor

The story of lay people in the church

by Geoffrey Barnes

Uniting Church Press
Melbourne

Published by
THE JOINT BOARD OF CHRISTIAN EDUCATION
Second Floor, 10 Queen Street, Melbourne 3000, Australia

THE FORGOTTEN FACTOR: the story of lay people in the church

© Geoffrey Barnes 1991

This publication is copyright. Other than for the purposes and subject to the conditions prescribed under the Copyright Act, no part of it may in any form or by any means (electronic, mechanical, microcopying, photocopying, recording or otherwise) be reproduced, stored in a retrieval system or transmitted without prior written permission from the publisher.

National Library of Australia
Cataloguing-in-Publication entry.

Barnes, Geoffrey, 1926–
    The forgotten factor: the story of lay people in the church.

Bibliography

ISBN 0 85819 823 1.

1. Laity – History. 2. Laity – Uniting Church – History. 3. Lay ministry – History. 4. Lay ministry – Uniting Church – History. I. Joint Board of Christian Education. II. Title.

262.15

First printed 1991

Acknowledgment: Publication of this book was assisted by a grant from the J. D. Northey Lecture Fund.

Design by Robina Norton
Typeset by JBCE on Ventura Publisher in Dutch (Times Roman)
Printed by Brown, Prior Anderson Pty Ltd   JB91/3089

Table of Contents

Chapter 1: The forgotten factor	7
The earliest church	12
The monastic protest	14
The rise of Christendom	16
Chapter 2: The rise and fall of the laity	19
The Reformers	20
The Puritans	25
The Evangelicals	28
Chapter 3: Triumph over silence: laywomen in the church	33
A new age movement	35
Medieval women	37
The hidden ones	39
The crusaders	41
Women in the Uniting Church	44
Chapter 4: Making the church whole	47
In ministry	48
In mission	50
In ecumenism	53
In theology	54
Bibliography	61

1.
The forgotten factor

The laity is essential to the church. It is strange that the laity should ever become the forgotten factor in the church's history.

In medieval times it is recorded that an inquirer asked a priest what was the position of a layperson in the church. The priest replied, 'the layman has two positions: he kneels before the altar; that is one. And he sits below the pulpit; that is the other'. The narrator said there was a third the priest had forgotten: the layman puts his hand in his purse.[1] All the gifts of the laity – material and spiritual – are vital in the church's life and witness.

Yet it was not until 1963 that Stephen Neill and Hans Ruedi-Weber edited *The Layman in Christian History* in which they said nothing like it had ever been written before. Hendrik Kraemer had written in 1958 on *A Theology of the Laity*; but Neill and Weber's book was the first general survey ever made of the history of the laity, though the writers did admit that it was not strictly competent to write a history of the laity because the church is 'the laos', the whole people of God. Given the date of their book we can also forgive the editors for merely noting that laymen includes laywomen. The editors of the history were responding to an initiative taken by the World

Council of Churches in which the laity was rediscovered as Christ's servants in the public sphere.

Then Ralph Morton and Mark Gibbs produced *God's Frozen People*, following it in 1971 with *God's Lively People* to remind the modern church that the laity represented a vast unused potential for Christian ministry in the world. Whether they be politicians, journalists, teachers, public servants, scientists, diplomats or simply citizens trying to play a responsible role in the democratic process, the primary bearers of the church's ministry are Christian believers as they live out their secular vocations with as much insight, integrity, courage and compassion as they can muster.

It is already apparent that a lively laity is crucial for the 1990s. The excitement of the theology of the laity in the 60s has passed. Fashionable theological talk is now about the ministry of the whole people of God; but these more recent developments are only fruitful, I believe, if they build upon the foundations begun in the 60s. It is important, first of all, to update our understanding of the history of the laity and to relate it to the present context, in our case the Uniting Church in Australia. The influential Anglican, Gregory Dix, with whom Uniting Church people would not see eye to eye on the ministry, was nevertheless right when he wrote in *The Apostolic Ministry* that the study of history has its value not so much in furnishing immutable, perhaps dangerously cramping, precedents from the past as in its power to illuminate the origins and therefore the real nature and terms of present questions.[2]

Secondly, we have all noticed that as the Uniting Church addresses the problems of our time, its pronouncements have not always gained full support, especially from the laity, giving rise to pleas that their voice be more carefully acknowledged and considered. Who speaks for the church is a question faced by all our synods and by the assembly. In a church that rejoices in its diversity, who speaks for the church is an urgent challenge. However, as David Gill once remarked, Christian witness-by-pronouncement leaves the ministry of the laity looking like a non-starter. A lively lay apostolate is essential if the people of God is to minister to contemporary society.[3]

Thirdly, as in all church unions, the problem of identity has emerged. What is distinctive about the Uniting Church? It seemed more satisfying to be able to say I am a Congregationalist, I am a Methodist, I am a Presbyterian, than to say now I am 'a Uniting'. The old names provided us with certain ready norms of belief and behaviour, for example, in relation to alcohol and gambling. In an age when information is the life-blood of meaningful action, Uniting Church lay people must have theological literature they can understand. In an age when data-banks are vital, they need access to programs that help them recognise their own distinctive roles. Excellent responses are coming from the Uniting Church Press, for example the recent *What Does Our Church Say?*

Fourthly, there was the moving plea of Sir Ronald Wilson at his installation as President in 1988. He asked the church to do more to help laymen and women in their life in the world. What the President has underlined is that in an increasingly secular world, not only is the rediscovery of the laity important; the question of how to order the church and her mission becomes more important.

It is not only a question of evangelism; it is also the skill of bringing the Christian perspective to bear upon the increasingly complex decisions many lay people have to make in their daily lives. It is not, especially since the 1960s, that we have ignored the essential place of the laity; it is that we have forgotten to provide the relevant support they need in order to be faithful witnesses to the presence of God in the places where they live and work. Andrew Dutney has written:

> In the Uniting Church we are big on 'lay ministry'. But 'lay ministry' has come to mean what lay people can do *in and for the church*. What lay people can do, and are doing, *in and for the world* has been largely overlooked.[4]

These lectures will not necessarily deal with all the complex issues that lay people face; yet they will provide some perspectives within which to ask the questions that will stimulate the church to order its life in such a way as better to fulfil the mission of the people of God.

In the Roman Catholic Church, it was Yves Congar who devoted his remarkable theological gifts to an appreciation of Catholic laity and who alerted Vatican 2 to a renewed understanding of the apostolate of the laity. A revised edition of his work in 1953, *Lay People in the Church*, was published in 1985.

Whereas Neill and Weber put emphasis on the role of the laity in the world, Congar goes further and asks what does the recognition of the apostolic calling of the laity in the world mean for the church, its hierarchy, liturgy and ministry. Former Methodists will rejoice to know that Congar, a convinced Roman Catholic, wrote that every faithful Christian can and ought to adopt the magnificent saying of John Wesley, 'I look upon all the world as my parish'.[5]

The Uniting Church in Australia is our particular point of reference in this story of lay people in the church and therefore we are also interested in the three denominational traditions that brought it into being. The Uniting Church also points us to the future because our faith is that a new appreciation of our traditional histories will enhance the unity to which we are called by our *Basis of Union*. Admittedly there are yet divisions among us, not least among the laity, yet they provide food for thought and challenge us to more pertinent historical reflection.

I am sensitive to a possible reaction from lay people that our concern ought to be with all the people of the Uniting Church, ordained as well as lay. Why place the burden on the laity? Certainly a battery of voices comes at the modern laity. Win souls, feed the hungry, praise God, fight human oppression, deepen spiritual life, renew the church, build as better society. Maybe it is because religion is too serious a business to be left to the clergy! So let us celebrate the laity.

However, the creative power of the laity cannot be realised if, in a modern version of Corinthian bickering, we continue to divide ourselves in ways that are so familiar: My faith is personal... My faith is public... I win souls... I do social action... I am a Baptist... I am a Catholic... I take Holy Communion sitting down... I commune on my knees. The mood of the church today is characterised, I believe, by a desire for a practical unity in the essential mission of the church. It is not characterised by an anti-clericalism. The desire that activates both clergy and laity today is that each fulfil their role and that God be glorified in the whole of life. Thus ministry that stems from basic beliefs is the urgent need of the hour. In that enterprise there is no place for clericalising the laity and laicising the clergy.

There is an eerie myth about a Greek innkeeper who invited many guests into his standardised beds. If guests were too small, they were racked and stretched until they fitted even if they died. If others were too big, they were cut down to size until they fitted. There were no king-size or queen-size beds. It is an eerie myth; yet useful to remember lest we forget the difference between the rich diversity that is welcome in the Christian community and the standardised notions of consumerism that plague us.

There is quite properly an emphasis today on the formation, indeed the professionalisation, of the ordained ministry, particularly in the sense that the minister's pastoral skills should be honed and duly recognised in a world crying out for spiritual therapies. Yet it must not be at the expense of depreciating the role of the laity: the implicit doctrinal competence of the laity, for example, in helping to articulate the faith in today's world. Nor should we be pre-occupied with the unimportant when the demands on the laity are of such magnitude. Education of the laity by the laity for the laity is a crying need. Winston Churchill liked to tell the story of the man who saved a drowning child. When the child was delivered safe home to his mother, she said: 'Where's Johnny's cap?'

Who are the laity? The adjective 'laikos' from 'laos' meaning people is not used in the New Testament. 'Laos' often is. This means that in the New Testament there is no distinction between lay people and clergy people. At the beginning of this century the historian, Harnack, made much of this and concluded that the earliest church was an undifferentiated community living under a charismatic regime.[6] New Testament scholars today seriously question Harnack's theory, though there are some who find the theory attractive because it appears biblical and therefore authoritative and simple – not concerned with 'Johnny's cap'.

A later historian, G. H. Williams, interpreting 1 Peter, has written that the early Christians did not think of themselves as 'an amorphous egalitarian fellowship' but as a priestly kingdom constituted as such by baptism, a baptism that included an anointing with oil formerly reserved for priests only.[7]

Clement of Rome at the end of the first century was probably the first to make the distinction as it came to be understood in the Christian tradition. He used 'ho laikos anthropos' to refer to the liturgical responsibilities of the lay people. In the secular thinking of Clement's time it had been used to distinguish people from their leaders. In appreciating the New Testament doctrine of gifts, there is a legitimate place for distinction between laity and leaders, though the church through the ages has often found it difficult to correlate the priesthood of all believers with the doctrine of spiritual gifts, stressing one to the exclusion of the other.

According to our *Basis of Union* the validity of such a distinction between laity and clergy is found not in the uncritical acceptance of a biblical blue-print as if church order were something fixed in heaven for all time. The biblical record, especially in its witness to the gospel of divine grace, is crucial; but it must be understood in the light of the church's tradition, which for us contains the Creeds, the Reformation Confessions, the evangelical witness of John Wesley's sermons and the work of contemporary scholars. Uniting Church people do have a responsibility to explore their history 'to save Johnny, if not his cap!'

How is it, given the biblical witness, that the laity and laity formation has so often been forgotten in the church's theological formulations and pastoral ministry? I propose to discuss this question in several stages: in this first lecture we will reflect on the church's story up to the time of the Reformation and in the second lecture we will consider the three traditions that go to make up the Uniting Church. In the third lecture the role of laywomen will be the theme and finally we will reflect on 'making the church whole'.

The earliest church

The New Testament affirms that lay people had significant roles in the liturgy, in organisation and in teaching (Acts 1:15; 1 Corinthians 14:16; 1 Peter 3:15). In worship the problem was not how to encourage participation, but order – how to order the rich variety of lay gifts, notably for the benefit of all present and hence Paul preferred the gift of prophetic interpretation rather than unintelligible tongues.

The right of the laity to elect their own leaders because it was sanctioned by the apostles was strongly asserted up until the beginning of the 4th century (see Acts 6:5). Even Clement of Rome writing about the year 96 A.D. in defence of the established clergy at Corinth, whom a new generation of gifted leaders had deposed, did not deny that right; but rather criticised the younger leaders' failure to acknowledge the exemplary ministerial life of the older leaders.

In his epistle, James had provided the basis for another constitutional right of the laity. 'Therefore confess your sins to one another that you may be healed. The prayer of a righteous person has great power in its effects' (James 5:16). The hearing of another's confession long survived as a lay prerogative.

Justin Martyr and Origen emerged in the second century as gifted lay teachers (see 1 Peter 3:15; Hebrews 8:11). Inevitably the contrast between them and poor, often indifferently educated people, who went about simply witnessing to their faith came to be painfully apparent. Yet we should note this emphasis on the lay teaching office, an office not always exclusively male, if we accept the evidence of Clement of Alexandria.[8]

Nor should we forget that standards of education in the ancient world were high and many were able to engage in quite sophisticated theological debate. When Cyril of Alexandria was on the way to defeating Nestorius, crowds of lay people demonstrated in the streets in favour of Cyril's doctrine. In 1990, in Britain there were no demonstrations about the Bishop of Durham and his radical views; but there were plenty of riots about Mrs Thatcher's poll-tax.

The lay teaching office was to persist strongly until the turn of the 5th century, reaching a climax in the West in the controversy between Augustine, bishop of Hippo in North Africa, and a lay monk from Britain, perhaps Ireland, Pelagius. He came to Rome and won a considerable following from the lay intelligentsia. Pelagius believed that Augustine's emphasis on the sovereignty of grace detracted from the integrity of the human will. Augustine believed that Pelagius put an exaggerated emphasis on human moral capacity. Pelagius's views have been described as the lay person's heresy par excellence.

Augustine no doubt read the signs of the times more carefully than Pelagius, though both were endeavouring to address the gospel to Roman society when that society was not really willing to make the necessary moral effort for reform. The Roman senatorial class was excessively wealthy.[9] This clash between bishop and layman was to be influential for more than a thousand years. Unfortunately it marked the end of the great lay teachers as the medieval tradition required that teachers of divinity be ordained.

Why did the exercise of the lay gifts in worship, order and teaching fail to persist? There are many reasons but two of them will be instructive for us. They were events that were fruitful at the time, but which many Protestant writers believe were the points at which the church went seriously wrong. Yet that is a simplistic and polemical approach and tends to ignore the deeper wisdom that history can teach us. We must try to be more discerning. The two events were the development of monasticism and the rise of Christendom.

The monastic protest

According to Athanasius, it was St Anthony who started the monastic movement. Christians left the affluent cities and became hermits in the deserts of Egypt. Born of wealthy parents about the year 250, Anthony grew up in a pious Christian household. In his very late teens both parents died and Anthony was consumed with desire to fight evil and achieve Christian perfection. He distributed his wealth to the poor, made proper provision for his young sister, and began to live the simple life of poverty, eventually retreating to the desert. Anthony never became a priest and to the end of his life always paid studious deference even to the youngest deacon.

Athanasius' *Life of Anthony* was to become one of the most widely read Christian books of the time and it popularised the monastic style of spirituality. This way of life was organised and institutionalised by Pachomius, a kind of John Wesley of the Desert Fathers. Pachomius was a conscientious objector to military service and if released promised to give his life in service to others. The sayings of the desert people were collected by John Cassian who in his late teens was also attracted to the ascetic life. Unlike Anthony, Cassian was eventually ordained in Rome where he found himself more in sympathy with Pelagius than with Augustine. He established two monasteries in Marseilles, one for men and one for women. It was Cassian, Louis Bouyer has written, who, more than any other writer, transmitted to the West the organisation and teaching of the monks of the desert.[10] It is believed now that John Wesley was much influenced by John Cassian's writings.

The monastic movements, spanning seventeen hundred years and encompassing solitaries like Mother Julian of Norwich and communities of men and women like Taize and Mother Teresa's Brothers and Sisters of Charity, have exercised an extraordinary influence on Western civilisation. It was the monks and nuns, Congar has written, who preserved the elements of culture, who educated princes and who literally formed Christendom, and therefore Europe, spiritually.[11] Why are these movements of importance in understanding the needs of the laity?

Imbued as we are with Martin Luther's rejection of the monasteries as the way to salvation and Protestant England's despoiling of them, it is hard not to conceive of them as clerical. In their origins they were the result of lay initiative. Even in the 13th century, it was the lay initiative of Francis who founded a new order. In almost an exact parallel to Anthony, Francis found he could no longer be at ease in his father's rich merchant household and believed he was called to devote his life to the poor. In the 20th century, Mother Teresa has attracted laymen and women to serve the poor in Calcutta.

Monasticism was a lay protest movement. In its origins it was a protest movement against affluent, pagan society and against standardisation in the church. Those who retreated to the desert preferred the Bible and the Holy Spirit to Creed and Logos theology. When in the years 260-303 the church lived in peace from persecution and the church grew in prestige and affluence, martyrdom as the supreme example of a life devoted to Christ had ceased to be an option. So to sensitive souls the ascetic life-style, the uncompromising pursuit of salvation away from the snares and delusions of city life, became the new martyrdom. The monks were thus the successors of the martyrs.

The hellenistic world provided some models for earnest Christians intent on spirituality. Their ascetic pursuit of perfection was shaped not so much by theological dogma as by platonic dualism: a view of the world held captive by a cosmic struggle between forces of good and evil. There was obviously the tendency to rate virginity higher than marital life, an attitude which is not in itself distinctively Christian. In other words the attraction of the ascetic life-style arose not only from the Bible; there were models to hand in the pagan context.

At the same time monastic life was such an effective protest and the gifts of its exponents seemed so Christlike that it was hard not to think that such spirituality was requisite for the Christian priest as well as the monk. The Council of Trent in the sixteenth century adopted monkish ideals for the training of parish priests. Hence, strangely, the clericalisation of the monastic vocations; not all secular priests in effect became monks; but monks encouraged by the hierarchy tended to take on the status and institutionalism of the church. The Jesuits, for example, put themselves entirely at the service of the papacy.

The truth is that there was both threat and promise in the lay protests that gave us monks and nuns. There was the threat of perpetuating ancient dualisms, of limiting the gifts of the laity to life in the monastic community and creating competition between monastics and the clergy as to the way of salvation. On the other hand, there was the promise of developing the diverse gifts adumbrated in the New Testament, of service to the poor, and of evolving creative disciplines to conserve the treasures of the gospel. In the circumstances, it was another event that locked both the threat and the promise into the history of the church. We must try to disentangle the threads of history in order to distinguish between threat and promise and thereby re-establish the rightful role of the laity.

The rise of Christendom

The adoption of the Christian faith by the Emperor Constantine at the beginning of the 4th century brought the influence of the laity in the church to a climax. Whatever we make of Constantine's conversion to Christianity, the fact remains that his legislative program virtually marked the end of persecution and enabled Christians more and more to give full expression to their faith. If it is true that many of the troubles of the church have stemmed from the Constantinian church/state relationship – it is also true that the first church historian, Eusebius, quite properly believed that the Constantinian settlement was cause for rejoicing. And remarkably the mainline reformers of the 16th century – Luther, Calvin, Zwingli – did not escape the Constantinian tradition; they envisaged no separation of church and state.

Under the new regime, the teaching of the Christian faith, as we have seen, became a highly respected office. It is to Constantine, head of state, in his desire for unity of belief, that we owe the Council of Nicaea and the writing of the Nicene Creed. There was a sense in which the Christian emperor in his lay office had the most powerful role in the church. In the West, though not in the East, there developed an ambivalence about the Christian monarch. It seemed that in such an office, priestly powers were needed and hence the anointing of the monarch which lives on in the English coronation ceremonies.

Barely a hundred years after the Roman Empire had reached its zenith under Constantine, the signs of its fall were apparent, a phenomenon that has fascinated the minds of many, not least Augustine, in his great work *The City of God*. When the Roman Empire fell before the barbarian invasion, paradoxically it was the church that survived and carried on much of the Roman organisation and institutionalism. It managed to convert many of the invaders. So it is foolish to interpret these events as being of the devil; there was a providence in them, though not without cost.

Many were influenced by a conviction of the Lord's imminent return and the collapse of the classical tradition to re-assert the importance of the ascetic way of life. Thus the church of the Dark Ages and beyond abounded in monasteries and monastic spirituality. It was a survival technique designed to maintain Christian spirituality and keep the demonic powers at bay. In concert with other influences already noted it meant that by the height of the Middle Ages there was no more fundamental division than that between clergy and laity.[12] Medieval times were not without protest; there was St Francis, whom we have already noted, and Peter Waldo, a layman with a passion for helping the poor. What other creative lay activity there must have been the Popes syphoned off into the Crusades.

In conclusion we must say that Christendom inevitably gave the church a triumphalist mentality. There is cause to be thankful that the principalities and powers of the ancient world were brought into subjection, that the cultural and spiritual treasures of the ancient world were preserved. Strangely, however, the ascendancy of the laity was eclipsed. The lay teaching office all but disappeared, the spirituality of the monks and nuns was circumscribed by the needs of educating priests, of church order and organisation. Creative lay initiatives were submerged for seemingly more urgent needs.

An exception proved the rule: Pope Gregory VII (himself a monk) looked on Duke Hugh of Burgundy as a deserter because he had gone into a monastery; he put himself first rather than the safety of his people, Gregory said.[13] Gregory had not forgotten the role of the laity; many had.

Notes
1. Congar, 1985, p. xv.
2. The Apostolic Ministry, p. 288.
3. Macquarrie, p. 88.
4. 'A Worldly Calling', *Ministry* 2/2 (1989), p. 7.
5. Congar, p. 366.
6. Congar, p. 4.
7. Neill & Weber, p. 53.
8. Neill & Weber, p. 44.
9. Neill & Weber, p. 76.
10. Bouyer, vol. 1, p. 500.
11. Congar. p. 405.
12. Neill & Weber, p. 111.
13. Congar, pp. 408-9.

2.
The rise and fall of the laity

While the history of the church in medieval times illustrates an increasing separation between clergy and laity, it is refreshing to know that of the one hundred and twenty-two Byzantine patriarchs, thirteen were elevated from the laity. Several were high-ranking civil servants and scholars. John Glykys, made patriarch of Cyprus in 1315, was excused the obligation that bishops must be monks because his doctors said he needed to eat meat. Apparently a carnivorous monk would not do, a carnivorous patriarch was all right! Regrettably, John's wife, in accordance with the rules, obligingly left him and entered a convent.[1]

The laity of early and medieval times found ways of asserting their role in the church; yet their distinctive ministry was often forgotten. Both the church and pagan society found it easier to conceive of the exercise of lay gifts in priestly ways. The promise of the free exercise of lay gifts seemed to threaten the cohesion and stability of the church's life, especially when the Roman Empire fell before the barbarians. Not surprisingly then, the church clung to the models of organisation and administration it had adopted from its Roman context.

In time it became an issue as to whether the church had betrayed its New Testament heritage. Reformers in 16th century Europe returned to the Bible to re-establish the church on its gospel foundations. In 17th century England, the Puritans fought for further reform, and in the 18th century, the evangelicals revealed that despite the reforming and purifying zeal of two centuries there was still the need to call the people to become alive to scriptural holiness and apply it to church and nation.

In our Australian context, reformers, puritans and evangelicals could refer to Presbyterians, Congregationalists and Methodists. Congregationalists (typically understood to be broadminded) might not relish being classed with Puritans; but that is because of modern connotations of the word Puritan. Still, by making these connections we can immediately begin to see the historic traditions that go to make up the Uniting Church. We can appreciate that the Uniting Church was more than an attempt to glue together three denominations; it was an expression of the calling to enter more fully into the life of the whole church from biblical times until now, and in particular to explore again our distinctive denominational traditions. In a real sense the task was not undertaken with a view to devaluing our respective denominational treasures. It was undertaken in order to give them a wider currency; to put them at the disposal of preaching the gospel and renewing the church.

For Uniting Church people there is refreshment for the journey ahead by taking note of the new work that has been done on our particular traditions. Yves Congar and Vatican 2 have brought refreshment for Roman Catholic laity. What renewing power is there for us in our Protestant, that is to say, in our reforming, puritan and evangelical traditions? So let us look at our three traditions.

The Reformers

One of Martin Luther's great biblical re-discoveries was the doctrine of the priesthood of all believers. It is surprising that in the ensuing centuries the laity often found it hard to break free of established modes of ministry. Yet we must try to elucidate what it was that Luther's renewed attention to the biblical doctrine did for the laity and how subsequent events were to shape the formation of the laity.

People of Luther's time, even educated people, were not accustomed to a literal approach to scripture. It had been argued long before (by Rhadinus) that people, clergy and prelates, were a divine order symbolically fixed, as it were, according to the monastic disciplines of spirituality (described by Pseudo-Dionysius) namely purgation, illumination and perfection. The idea of prelates being perfect, of clergy being illumined and the people being purged is offensive to our minds. Yet for the medieval mind to abolish the difference and order of the members was to strike at the very being of society, its order and beauty.[2] Erasmus, that prince of humanists, made great fun of prelates and monks in an attempt to help his contemporaries see things differently. Another of his weapons was to teach the need of taking the meaning of the New Testament in literal, rather than allegorical, terms.

Luther proposed what the contemporary theologian, David Tracey, might call a paradigm shift in theology, a way of relating the authority of scripture to church and people unheard of for centuries. One can understand that at the time the statement that all Christians were literally kings and priests before God was not very acceptable to either church or state hierarchy. Of course there was a sense in which Luther also understood the 'royal priesthood' of the New Testament figuratively. He did not mean that all Christians should literally wear crowns and celebrate Mass at the altar. He did mean that if status related to function, it followed from the function and not the other way around. The medieval notion of order meant that function flowed from status.

The given order of things did not only apply to the church. It applied to secular society as well. We must not assume, therefore, that in the sixteenth century the church usurped the role of monarchs and princes. Since the time of Constantine, the church had developed notions of the ecclesiastical competence of secular rulers. The emperor, Constantine, had called the Council of Nicaea; Sigismund, Holy Roman emperor, had called the Council at Constance. Remarkably, not until Lateran V was it decreed that only a pope could call a church council.

But Luther went further, proposing the doctrine of emergency whereby lay rulers might take matters into their own hands and deal with corruption in the church. When the rebellious peasants took things into their own hands, Luther faced a dilemma in which even he failed to apply the new paradigm. He reverted to the medieval position where the lay ruler's role was to preserve the divinely ordained order. Once again, not all the chains that bound the laity could be shaken off.

Though Luther was not good at practical or political theology, and though his doctrine of the priesthood of all believers was perverted by later Protestantism in 'an atomistic and naively anti-clerical sense', we should not be unaware of its importance for the laity then and now.[3] In his famous sermon at the dedication of the Castle Church at Torgau, many years after the Peasants' Revolt (1524-26), the doctrine of universal priesthood enunciated in the manifestoes of the 1520s still shines through:

> Rather we are all priests, as is written in 1 Peter 2:9; so that all of us should proclaim God's word and works at every time and in every place, and persons from all ranks, races, and stations may be specially called to the ministry, if they have the grace and the understanding of the scriptures to teach others.[4]

In principle, for Luther, the distinction between 'clergy' and 'laity' fell away.

John Calvin's great theological work, *Institutes of the Christian Religion*, began as the work of a lay person. For Calvin, as for Luther, the Bible was the mediator of new life in Christ. 'For we who are defiled in ourselves', Calvin wrote, 'yet are priests in him'.[5] If there is any difference between Luther and Calvin it is that while Luther allows that by grace we are all made worthy as priests to stand face to face with God and pray for others, Calvin, being opposed to any suggestion that believers can supplement the once for all sacrifice of Christ, practically dispenses with priesthood all together. Christ in his humanity is our high priest; there can be no other.

Calvin argued in Book IV of the *Institutes* that the church in its history had been deflected from organising itself in accordance with its original gospel and he lays down the Pauline principle that in the church all things should be done with 'decency, love and a free conscience'.[6] R. S. Paul has described this as an extremely important practical principle.[7] It is Calvin's acknowledgment that there is not only need for flexibility in church order but that provision for the diversity of gifts in the church is the politically appropriate expression of love.

So if Calvin dispenses with the priestly concept in relation to believers, he certainly does not dispense with the ordered ministry of the laity. As it turned out Calvinism created a more militant laity than Lutheranism not least because of the strong link created between Calvinism and democracy. Lutheranism created striking lay individuals; in Calvinism lay activity is not so much the activity of the individual as the corporate witness of a community. It helps to explain the importance of the congregation for Presbyterians and Congregationalists.

This emphasis needs to be made because Calvin's understanding of the place of the laity is frequently misunderstood. He has been accused of instigating the Protestant oppression of the laity, of a doctrine of ministerial order that left little freedom of conscience to the laity. Certainly there must be good order in church and society: both Luther and Calvin shared the medieval horror of disorder; but Calvin explains more carefully than Luther how that order is to be expressed.

Where there was explicit direction in the New Testament, Calvin believed it must be followed – for example there must be ministers, there must be sacraments – other details, Calvin believed, depended on the state of the times.[8]

Like Luther, Calvin had to do his theology in context and given the situation in Geneva, he had to work out a more detailed plan of preachers, teachers, elders and deacons. Yet this was not to be understood as a divinely ordered system. Later Calvinists were not so careful to allow flexibility in church order (see The Westminster Confession) and it was to lead to many debates in the next century. As George Yule has reminded the Uniting Church, the eldership was not originally Scottish: it derived from Martin Bucer of Strassburg with whom Calvin was closely acquainted. Calvin introduced it at Geneva perhaps because it appealed to the magistrates as a way of maintaining order in the community. It must also be seen, however, as Calvin's application of the pastoral principle that things be done decently and in order.

Whether the ruling elders, that is those concerned with discipline as distinct from the teachers and pastors, are strictly lay is somewhat ambiguous in Calvin. That the eldership became a feature of Scottish church life and thus it was transmitted to Australia is cause for rejoicing. It can be seen as a valuable tradition celebrating lay gifts that we can develop in our own context.

The fiery Scot, originally a Catholic priest, John Knox was responsible for transmitting Calvinism to Scotland. A time in the galleys after the defeat of the Scottish lords at St Andrew's by the French Catholics was not designed to lessen his fiery Protestant temperament. It was Knox, Gordon Rupp has declared, who sensed the revolutionary implications of Calvin's doctrine. Writing a letter to the Commonalty of Scotland, Knox declared:

> I would ye should esteem the reformation and care of religion no less to appertain to you, because ye are no kings, rulers, judges, nobles nor in authority. Beloved brethren ye are God's creatures... and this is the point wherein I say, all man is equal.[9]

In effect this is saying what Luther had said, that the laity has the responsibility to reform the church. Hence the appeal of Knox to the Scottish lords and the formation of Protestant congregations in which we should note that Holy Communion was celebrated by Knox, not by lay persons. Knox did not confuse the doctrine of the priesthood of all believers as an 'undifferentiated community living under a charismatic regime'.[10]

When it came to translating the insights of the Reformation into documents that would help to guarantee its continuance and recognition by civil authorities, the freedom and flexibility that the reformers believed pertained to the laity were not fully spelt out. There was a very good theological reason for this: the gifts and graces of the laity were not, as we have seen, to be fixed in any kind of order for all time. Though, of course, it was important to define the nature of the ordained ministry and its relation to civil authority. Civil leaders were very sensitive at the point of possible social disorder and the uprising at Munster in 1535 by radical, unlettered, would-be reformers gave some justification for their caution.

George Yule was responsible for persuading the Joint Commission on Church Union to include in its allegiance to the English and Scottish Reformation confessions the Heidelberg Catechism. Both Luther and Calvin had seen the need of catechisms to educate and form the younger generation in Protestant spirituality. The Heidelberg Catechism, however, is, for us in the Uniting Church, unique in that it is not English or Scottish, and more especially it is a remarkable blend of continental Lutheranism and Calvinism. It therefore reminds us of our Protestant roots in the continental reformation.

Yet more particularly it does acknowledge the place and role of the laity in a beautiful answer to the question:

Q. 55: What do you understand by 'communion of saints'?
A: First that all believers one and all, as partakers of the Lord Christ, and all his treasures and gifts, shall share in one fellowship. Second, that each one ought to know that he is obliged to use his gifts freely and with joy for the benefit and welfare of other members.[11]

The Scots Confession of 1560 has a similar emphasis on the church as the communion of saints (chapter XVI) and thus the reformers sought to celebrate the place and role of the laity in the church. We must turn now to the English Puritans and in so doing we will refer to some of the Reformation confessions in the *Basis of Union* of the Uniting Church.

The Puritans

Hitherto we have been considering the Reformers with special attention to John Calvin and the rise of Scottish Presbyterianism. Now we turn to the English Puritans who are the originators of Congregationalism.

Recent historical studies, notably by Patrick Collinson at one time Professor of History at Sydney University, strongly underline the fact that we ought not to look for a clear-cut emergence of Congregationálism in the 16th century in the sense of a denomination as we understand it in the 20th century. It is truer to say that there was a variety of groups in the 16th century seeking purification or reform of the English church. Such groups were not uninfluenced by Martin Luther and John Calvin; but they also espoused some of the views of radical movements on the continent.

Robert Browne, a somewhat erratic churchman of the 16th century, was one of those influenced by his association on the continent with radical or anabaptist groups. Sometimes known as the father of separatist Congregationalism, he believed that the Church of England was no church and therefore Christians ought to separate themselves from it. Browne nevertheless wrote:

> The church planted or gathered is a company or number of christians or believers, which by a willing covenant made with their God, are under the government of God and Christ, and keep his laws in one holy communion: because Christ hath redeemed them unto holiness and happiness for ever, from which they were fallen by the sin of Adam.[12]

Here was a definition of the church that really did not conceive of church membership as an optional extra for Christian laity; nor, despite its author's categorisation as a Separatist, did it in its intention seek to destroy the unity of the one, holy, catholic and apostolic church. It is not surprising, perhaps, that the church as 'a company gaddred or assembled together of true and faythful christen people' by the Holy Spirit under the headship of Christ first appeared in a catechism of the Strassburg reformer, Wolfgang Capito.[13] Nor is it surprising that so called non-separatist Congregational Puritans should adopt a similar definition.

What is of more than passing interest is that such a definition emphasises that the laity is of the essence of the church. In the 17th century, many Congregational or Independent churches were to come into being through lay initiative, embodied in a covenant relationship, before a minister or pastor was called. The ordained ministry was not therefore of the 'essence' of the church; though the Savoy Declaration of 1658 makes it abundantly clear that the ordained ministry was far from being considered irrelevant.[14] Strangely, in New England where Congregationalist immigrants established what amounted to a theocracy administered by the congregation, the ordained ministers constituted a powerful body. Despite later developments, Congregationalists have always held strongly to the congregation as a covenanted fellowship for the ordering of lay gifts. Robert Paul has remarked that Congregationalists tend to remain fundamentalists in matters of polity long after they have ceased to be fundamentalist in anything else.[15]

The divines of the Westminster Assembly had some protracted debates on church polity. The Scots commissioners believed that Presbyterianism was divinely ordained while the Congregational delegates believed the same of Congregationalism. On nearly all the important theological issues there was agreement, hence the similarity between the Westminster and Savoy Declarations. On the question of polity the Assembly issued a separate document on the form of government. Those who disagreed with the document, the Dissenting Brethren (Congregationalists), issued *An Apologeticall Narration*, and at Savoy similarly a separate chapter on polity was issued. On the eldership, *An Apologeticall Narration* declared:

> For Officers and publique Rulers in the Church, we set up no other but the very same which the reformed Churches judge necessary and sufficient, and as instituted by Christ and his Apostles for the perpetuall government of his Church, that is, *Pastors, Teachers, Ruling Elders*, (with us not lay but Ecclesiastique persons separated for that service) and *Deacons*.[16]

It is noteworthy that such was the difference of opinion among the Puritans on church government that it was not possible to write Presbyterianism or Congregationalism into a Confession. In spite of themselves, the Westminster divines showed wisdom in not making church organisation an article of faith.

Yet still we argue the merits of this or that way of ordering the gifts of the church as if there were some divinely detailed blueprint for it, whereas the early Protestant reformers at least were sufficiently true to the scripture to be very wary of any such prescription. They were equally well aware, however, that although all believers are priests, all believers are not ordained ministers.[17] Calvin and the reformers, insisting on Christ as the one true priest, were pleading that the only true theology is where the church takes priority, yet not in an arbitrary or rigid way. This acknowledgment provides the proper context for any Protestant theology of ministry, both lay and ordained.

The rediscovery of the laity in reformed and puritan churches was soon lost in a plethora of polemics in which inevitably the educated ministry had most of the say. The Reformation stressed the need of an educated ministry, the Puritans placed great store by careful biblical exegesis; yet the pressure of the Counter-Reformation and the diversity of Puritan ideas of the church demanded the knowledge and skills of educated leaders rather than the simple faith of the laity. As Patrick Collinson has recently pointed out, this situation in post-Reformation Britain has predisposed many earlier historians to concentrate on doctrinal history so that many scenes from clerical life are under-explored, to say nothing of the laity. How, for example, did pastoral visits interact with the habits and rhythms of hospitality? 'Would the threatened visit of the minister lead to an onslaught on household dirt, as in modern Scotland?'[18]

The Evangelicals

We must turn now to the Evangelicals to see how once more the creative gifts of the laity were to re-emerge. I have always felt that the evangelical revival in the English speaking world represents the full flowering of English Puritanism. The forbears of the Wesleys were Puritans and the American revival owed much to Jonathan Edwards who was of Puritan stock.[19] I see Methodism as a blossoming of many of the positive elements of Puritanism. It is a vital part of the evangelical revival that included Whitfield and the Countess of Huntingdon, Jonathan Edwards, William Wilberforce and the Clapham Sect. Regardless of doctrinal differences, they all devoutly believed that the gospel of grace must be addressed to all people.

On the continent, a new piety surfaced that greatly influenced the revivals in England and America. In reaction to a rigid Lutheranism, two German theologians, Francke and Spener, developed a spirituality that emphasised the validity of lay experience. It was a development influenced by the Enlightenment which by exalting human reason reduced the prestige of the clergy and implied that lay people could be enlightened. It was a remarkable experiment in spirituality which encouraged people to record their experiences much as the Puritans had done.

When the Reformation Christians were forced out of Moravia (Czechoslovakia), they found refuge in Germany on the estate of Count Nikolaus von Zinzendorf. He was a layman, a Lutheran pietist, with high flown ambitions. He was somewhat eccentric, though he was ably assisted by his wife who actually managed the economic life of the community at Herrnhut. It was this community that John Wesley (1703-91) visited and it was therefore the Moravians who were the vehicles of John Wesley's conversion. In a remarkable way, three great streams of spirituality converge with John Wesley – reformed, puritan and evangelical.

In principle the Wesleyan movement in England was highly clerical. Practically, Stephen Neill has written, 'it was the greatest organisation for the employment of lay forces that has ever existed'.[20] Initially Methodism did not grant full participation of the laity in the government of the church. The first itinerant preachers were lay people who eventually met in annual conference.

The liberation of the laity within Methodism was both threat and promise. Wesley had written that it might be possible after his death for all preachers to meet together and determine matters by vote. In the meantime he insisted that all preachers serve him as 'sons in the Gospel'.[21] It was the later lay-led movements, the New Connexion (1797), the Bible Christians (1816), the Primitive Methodists (1811), the United Methodist Free Churches (1857) that put the emphasis on the laity more strongly. The Independent Methodists insisted that there should be no distinction between clergy and laity, between men and women. The Primitives permitted women lay preachers. Dinah Morris in the novel *Adam Bede* was inspired by the Primitives. The United Free Methodists campaigned strongly for lay representation in church government.

Separation from the Church of England, or from parent Methodism, inevitably pre-disposed the preachers to take on pastoral responsibilities in relation to the societies they brought into being. In time, local preachers became professionalised pastors. Itinerant preachers and evangelists were obliged to act like bishops. It was they who constituted the annual conference Wesley had envisaged and which, in time, became the supreme legislative body of the Methodist Connexion in England; dare I say, the corporate archbishop!

Still in local religious societies and in the community Methodist lay people were remarkably active. They represented a great potential for the employment of lay gifts in the church. In the early years of the Methodist Annual Conference, however, we see again the tendency for the exercise of lay gifts to be subsumed into the clerical mode.

Sadly we must conclude that in the early days of the Reformation there breathed the spring freshness of the re-discovery of the ministry of the laity. Later the harsh autumn winds of polemic blew and lay ministries tended to be frozen into static forms. In England, the Anglican monarchy forced the Puritans into dissent and thus Puritan legalism was born of Anglican regalism.

The evangelical revival promised a new beginning, indeed many notable lay persons decisively influenced the course of history, such as the Countess of Huntingdon, Hannah More, William Wilberforce and Robert Raikes. Still lay initiative became clericalised yet again when the genius of the Wesleys was, of necessity, translated into the Methodist Connexion. What happened in Methodism was certainly not a disaster. Methodists have contributed mightily, for example, by their insistence on the place of lay preachers in the church.

In the 1990s, we need to prepare for the 21st century. To gain the right perspective for that vital enterprise we need to look back over the past two hundred years. We must remember our Reformation and evangelical history with all the passion that brings us a sense of identity and an understanding of why things happened as they did. And we must remember it with all the critical skill that will enable us to celebrate our past, but not to repeat it.

Notes

1. Sheils & Wood, pp. 142-3.
2. Sheils & Wood, p. 162.
3. Neill & Weber, p. 139.
4. *Luther's Works*, vol. 51, p. 335.
5. *Institutes*, II.xv.6.

6. *Institutes*, IV.x.27-32.
7. Paul, *Freedom with Order*, p. 22.
8. *Institutes* IV.x.30.
9. Neill & Weber, p. 140.
10. Congar, p. 4.
11. Paul, p. 27.
12. Peel and Carlson, p. 253. Reprinted by permission of Harper Collins Publishers.
13. Rupp, p. 116.
14. Rupp, p. 119.
15. Paul, *Freedom with Order*, p. 33.
16. Paul, *Apologeticall Narration*, p. 8.
17. Manson, p. 69.
18. Sheils & Wood, p. 191.
19. Rupp, p. 450.
20. Neill & Weber, p. 206.
21. Davies & Rupp, p. 276.

3.
Triumph over silence: laywomen in the church

If the layman has been the forgotten factor in the history of the church, it is even more strongly the case that the laywoman has been forgotten. It is the more remarkable, notwithstanding the injunction in 1 Timothy 2:12 that women are to keep silent in church, when both from scripture and from tradition it is clear that women are richly endowed with pastoral gifts.

We will have to explore the history of the church, not to prove that throughout the centuries there have been remarkable Christian women, because modern scholarship now abounds with biographies of such women; we must explore the history of the church to understand why laywomen were given a subordinate place and thereby learn to tell the story differently in the future. In other words, we study the church's history in order to understand the present and claim the promise of the future.

In 1958, Hendrik Kraemer was the guest lecturer at Westminster College, Cambridge. While there he delivered the Hulsean Lectures on *A Theology of the Laity* to which we have already referred. He said in a section entitled 'Women – Fully part of the Laity':

> There is... no subject on which the Christian church has always been (and in most cases still is) so retrograde, so subject to non-Christian, pagan notions of the sexes and to patriarchal thinking as in regard to women and their place in the church.[1]

Kraemer alerts us here not only to the importance of the issue; he also implies that non-Christian factors have <u>unduly</u> influenced the Christian understanding of the place of women laity. He emphasises, therefore, the need for Christians to understand what has happened to bring about this situation.

Since Kraemer made that statement, it is good to be able to say that extraordinarily interesting work has been done. As yet there is no full consensus across the ecumenical board, for example on the ordination of women. However, what has emerged is a vital and scholarly interest in the biblical record about the status of women. In the long run, that cannot help but be a sign of hope.

In a recent book, *Women in the Earliest Churches*, Ben Witherington has argued:

> It appears that the New Testament evidence shows a definite tendency on the part of the authors addressing the earliest church to argue for or support by implication the new freedom and roles women may assume in Christ. At the same time, the evidence indicates an attempt at reformation, not repudiation, of the universal patriarchal structure of family and society in the first century in so far as it included the Christian family and community.[2]

If, having surveyed the recent writing on this subject, Ben Witherington is right, then we may safely conclude that 'in Christ' a new role and freedom for women have come into being by the preaching of the gospel. This is especially the case as compared with the societies contemporary with the New Testament. Witherington also makes it clear that the patriarchal structure of society was so pervasive that the New Testament witness is inevitably shaped by that patriarchal context.

When from our perspective we interpret the scriptures it is obviously incumbent on us to appreciate that context. We should not expect the apostle Paul to emerge from the pages of the Bible looking like an honorary feminist. Witherington does not go as far as Phyllis Trible and say that 'since new occasions teach new duties, so contexts alter texts, liberating them from frozen construction'.³ I agree with Witherington that if contexts are allowed to alter texts radically, then historical perspective is lost, and what writers of the New Testament were actually saying at the time regrettably becomes unimportant.

Why was it that the liberation for women that the New Testament promised failed to materialise more quickly? To answer that we need first of all to move beyond the earliest churches to the churches of the period after the New Testament up until the Council of Nicaea in 325. In that time Christianity outgrew its Palestinian context and became established at the heart of the Graeco-Roman world. At the Council, the emperor, Constantine, having officially recognised the Christian faith, wished to ensure that his empire was not torn apart by divisions within the church itself. Thus the Nicene Creed came into being to become one of the ways in which we express today our unity with Christians across the world. It also focuses for us the new context within which to understand Christianity.

A new age movement

As Christianity took more solid root in the Roman world, it encountered the prevailing religions and philosophies of the time. Christians, as persecutions from time to time cruelly revealed, could not live their lives in a vacuum. Inevitably the culture of the times influenced their spirituality.

One of the most popular religions was gnosticism, a kind of new age movement that promised salvation by way of the right knowledge. Attune yourself to the right vibrations and you will be all right. It proposed marvellously coloured philosophies by which to live. Elizabeth Schussler Fiorenza in *In Memory of Her*, has helped us see how these popular philosophies perhaps enhanced Christianity's view of a new role for women. Valentinian gnosticism, for example, saw no opposition between male and female. Some scholars, though, think that the removal of the separation between male and female is more like re-absorption of the female principle into the male one.[4]

In an earlier book, *The Gnostic Gospels* by Elaine Pagels, we might be forgiven for thinking that gnosticism provided all the right vibrations needed for a celebration of the feminine gifts of the Spirit, and much more importantly, that the church made a terrible mistake in opposing gnosticism so strongly. Some have gone so far as to say the reason the church rejected gnosticism was because of the prominence it gave to women. Witherington believes that there is insufficient evidence to show that this is the reason for the church's rejection. Fiorenza has written that gnosticism was itself not free of patriarchalism. To have adopted gnosticism as the way to celebrate women's gifts would have been to escape the frying pan for the fire.

In the writings of Irenaeus towards the end of the second century, gnosticism was rejected because it detracted from the belief that the Christian good news for women and men was rooted in the life and blood events of history. Irenaeus convinced the church that Christianity was not mysterious philosophies, a new age movement; it was good news passed on crystal clear by the apostles; it was not the denial of this world, but the promise of its fulfilment, its liberation. What threatened the church was the accent the new age philosophies gave to a separation between body and spirit. In fighting that battle, emphasis was put on the apostles, all men, and on historic facts that minimalised what good, if any good at all, might come from gnosticism.

Did the church make the right response in the circumstances? Given the context in which it lived, yes, I believe it did. Irenaeus took the question back to the apostles and to scripture thereby preserving the historic witness of Jesus to the essential ministry of women. Gnosticism may have been some temporary gain, yet in the end the new light that shines from the gospel might have become illusory.

The early church was not bereft of popular gurus. Prophets were major figures. The school of the prophet, Montanus, brought to prominence two women, Prisca and Maximilla. Like gnosticism, montanism was also condemned. Was it because of the two prophetesses or because when Montanus died, Maximilla became the leader of the group? Yes, we would have to admit that the church leaders did respond in a patriarchal way;

Hippolytus called them 'wretched women', and Origen, an otherwise great theologian, was not much better.

There was another issue at stake, however. The rise of a charismatic school of prophets purporting to speak in the name of the Spirit and provide new revelations from God was a challenge to the authority of the institutional church. It was a classic case of what can be called 'Spirit versus structure'. We can acknowledge the patriarchalism involved; but we must also be aware of the theology involved because Spirit filled utterances that seem to call in question the fullness of revelation in Jesus Christ need to be very carefully weighed. Still we must not quench the Spirit and it was a pity that, because of the condemnation, all the books of Montanus were burned in 298. So ever since we can only read of Montanism through approved, polemical sources.[5]

Overall we must admit that gnosticism and montanism, creating as they did crises of faith, took their toll of the role of laywomen. The church found it difficult to be flexible and the more so because it was not altogether wrong in questioning the theology of Montanus. One response at the time on the part of women was to retreat into the desert and, as we have seen, there was both gain and loss for the laity in the monastic movement.

Medieval women

Queen Etheldreda in England married twice. Retaining her virginity, she in due course left her second husband and founded an abbey on the Isle of Ely in the middle of the fens not far from Cambridge. The foundation was actually a double community, one for monks and one for nuns, though the abbess, Etheldreda, was really in charge of both, reflecting thereby the Celtic influence on Anglo-Saxon Christianity. It was the Roman influence which insisted on more separation between male and female in monastic communities. At Ely, the male community being at hand meant, of course, that priests were readily available to say Mass for the nuns.

In a short time Etheldreda became famous for her piety and attracted wealth and fame to her abbey. When she died, she was succeeded as abbess by her sister whose name, believe it you must, was Sexburga and who was equally famed for her spirituality. The place is now marked by the magnificent Ely Cathedral which with its architecturally superb lantern tower rises from the fens like a glorious ship.

For a thousand years from the time of Constantine, the context for Christianity was medieval Christendom. Barbarian invasions from the North prevented new initiatives in lay theology, though the church was not unsuccessful in winning the barbarians for Christ who themselves left their mark on the church. Yet they did not change the role of women as understood by Roman Christianity. In winning the Barbarians, the church found itself perpetuating the pagan submission of women.

That is not to say that in medieval times remarkable women did not emerge and contribute significantly to Christian faith and witness. Recent books inspired by the feminist movement are making that abundantly clear. Etheldreda and Sexburga are cases in point, though they illustrate what we have already noted that they cannot break free of the prevailing monastic modes of spirituality.

One of the most remarkable women of medieval England was Margery Kempe whose book, dictated to a priest in the 14th century, was discovered in the 1930s. Margery was a pioneer in the art of keeping a spiritual journal, albeit telling her stories rather than writing them. She and Julian of Norwich were acquainted; but whereas Julian allowed the church to enclose her and live a life of comparative solitude as an anchoress, Margery, despite her marriage, thirteen children and a brewery to manage, betrothed herself to Christ and used her gift of tears on every possible occasion to make for her a sacrament of unity with Christ. She made many pilgrimages; yet she never became a nun or a recluse. Margery was essentially a laywoman of no great education, struggling to give expression to her gifts in a world that ere long would change dramatically.

The Book of Margery Kempe will not stand comparison with the haunting revelations of Mother Julian, the first truly great English woman of letters, the woman theologian par excellence; but it is important that Margery's story be told because in her simple way she bears witness to the validity of a medieval laywoman's experience of the divine.

The hidden ones

What recent historical studies are doing is to bring to light the stories of what the American Puritan, Cotton Mather, called 'the hidden ones'. In so doing, the hidden contribution of women to the reform of the church becomes apparent. We are led to dig beneath the surface of the theology taught by the reformers to find that there were other more feminine motivations and influences present.

There is still some debate as to whether Martin Luther was essentially a medieval or a modern person. When he wrote...

> A woman must be a woman and cannot be a man. She, too, is God's creature and her divine station is that she should bear and care for children. So I am a man, created for another office and work. But should I be proud because of this and day: I am not a woman, therefore, I am better in the sight of God? Should I not rather praise God for creating both the woman and me also through the woman and putting me in this station? What an un-Christian things it is that one should despise another because he is in another station or is doing something other than he is doing[6] ...

perhaps we will conclude that his outlook is medieval because of the emphasis on station or status.

Yet the seeds of a revolution in women's status had been sown. Luther acknowledged that every lay person's calling whether in the home or in society was a holy calling. There was no need to go to a monastery to find one's eternal salvation. There was just as much holiness and assurance of salvation in a loving marriage as in ploughing the fields or in crafting brewers' barrels. Indeed many monks and nuns forsook their monasteries. Katherine von Bora left the nunnery but could find no-one to marry. She proposed to Father Martin Luther and he, declaring that he was not a sexless stone, accepted her.

As a result the Protestant home, in Roland Bainton's apt phrase, 'the school for character' was established at the heart of Protestant spirituality. Luther had not escaped the notion of marriage as a remedy for sin, a notion enshrined in Cranmer's Anglican Prayer Book. Still no nunneries meant an end of a world-denying, flesh-denying spirituality for Protestant women.

Scottish John Knox, having experienced Calvin's church in Geneva as the most perfect school of Christ on earth, seems unduly to exaggerate. His experience of Mary, Queen of Scots, and Catherine de Medici of France led him to pen *The First Blast of the Trumpet against the Monstrous Regiment of Women*, a document of which Elizabeth I heartily disapproved. Calvin, it is true, did not use the vulgar proverb that Eve was the 'well spring of the mischief that befell mankind'; both Adam and Eve were guilty, he declared, though he felt that if a woman were not subject to her husband there would be no order left in nature. Nevertheless to his credit he did require after 1536 that all children, girls as well as boys, should attend school.[7]

The reformers were men of their time. They could not be otherwise. In the case of women, their new literal emphasis on the Bible confirmed them in much medieval prejudice. The most perfect school of Christ did not give equal status to women, nor promise liberation like to that of men. The anabaptist or radical wing of the Reformation, no less literal in its approach to scripture and no less free of patriarchalism, was notable for the number of women leaders who came to prominence. Hundreds of them were martyred in the 16th century by Protestants and Catholics alike. They went to their deaths declaring their joy at the prospect of meeting the celestial bridegroom. It was hard for simple lay people, albeit of radical views, to articulate their faith in such dire circumstances without recourse to medieval models of spirituality.

When denouncing the rebels in south-western England, Archbishop Thomas Cranmer referred to foolish women who 'commonly follow superstition rather than true religion', and admittedly there were some whose superstition was of the old Catholic kind. Yet research recently done on wills suggests that, although women at the time did not commonly make wills, there may be some significance in the fact that they contain a lower proportion of bequests to traditional Catholic purposes than do their male equivalents.[8] Perhaps women did more for radical Protestantism than men. John Bunyan's church at Bedford was established (1650) by eight women and four men.[9]

In 17th century England, it seems that women found in the sectarian or dissenting congregations the opportunity to move into untraditional modes of religious expression. While not permitted to preach in the congregation, they were encouraged to prophesy, that is to speak of their understanding of a passage of scripture and how it related to their lives. Such freedom was not allowed in the Church of England where women were required, Mary Astell said, 'to know their catechism and a few good Sentences, to read a Chapter and say their Prayers, though perhaps', she continued, 'with as little understanding as a Parrott'.[10]

The conventions of the dissenting churches (mostly Baptist and Congregational) provided women with a sense of belonging, even of excitement, in the Christian faith. In other words, the non-Anglican congregations had a structure, if not always an articulated theology, that acknowledged the laywoman's gifts. Women were no longer required to be silent. The recent, more sociological approach to the writing of Protestant history, rather than one dependent on the writings of the leaders, is much more able to trace the contribution of women.

The crusaders

The next great movement in the story of laywomen was the evangelical revival. Evangelical preaching encouraged everyone to find in their own religious experience a pathway to personal salvation and liberation. So women often joined the church alone, that is without the support of their husbands.[11] Women banded themselves together in organisations because they were otherwise excluded from the governing bodies of their churches. The Methodist Episcopal women in America published *The Heathen Woman's Friend*, a title which reflects its time, though in another sense it is a recognition of the unique gifts women bring to the Christian mission.

'Pope Joan' is a name given to Selina, the Countess of Huntingdon (1717-1791) by her detractors because of her influence in the Whitfield branch of Methodism. The Countess is a good illustration of the way in which evangelicalism opened up exciting possibilities for women. Estimates of the wisdom of some of the Countess's philanthropic ventures, especially in America, vary, though it is difficult not to fall under her spell when one encounters her remarkable work. Being the widow of an earl, she had the means to promote and endow revivalistic enterprises. Selina stands like Etheldreda, abbess of Ely, in a tradition in which aristocratic women sponsored religious and educational institutions.

The Lady Selina was drawn towards the Methodists by her sisters-in-law, the Ladies Elizabeth and Margaret Hastings. Margaret in fact married a Methodist preacher, Benjamin Ingham. Selina invited her noble friends to her drawing room to hear George Whitfield. They included such raddled old sinners as the Duchess of Marlborough. 'God knows', the Duchess said, 'we all need mending, and none more than myself'.[12] The Countess thus took the evangelical revival into high places where the Wesleys had no entree.

Friends and admirers of the Countess found that she was not always easy to get on with. In a day when lords were lords and ladies were ladies, Selina rather expected that everyone should do her bidding without question. She wanted to establish chapels and run them within the Church of England with evangelical clergymen of her choosing. That did not fit in with the Anglican system. Again we find how difficult it was for lay initiative to transform the traditional structures. Sadly Selina wrote, 'I am to be cast out of the Church of England, only for what I have been doing these forty years – speaking and living for Jesus Christ'.[13] Here is a woman, somewhat eccentric by our standards, perhaps like Margery Kempe, struggling to give expression to her religious experience in a context that was alien to it. Nor was it just the Anglican establishment that proved difficult; organised Methodism took a long time to give to laywomen the same rights it gave to laymen in church government.

In David Edward's *Christian England*, there is an interesting chapter entitled 'Unconventional Victorians' in which he discusses women as crusaders, namely Elizabeth Fry, Florence Nightingale and Josephine Butler, all great humanitarian leaders. They liberated not only the victims of sordid evils, but in so doing, Edwards has written, they liberated themselves.

Elizabeth Fry came of a Quaker family and she married a Quaker, Joseph Fry. Elizabeth was upset when the Quaker community to which she belonged expelled her husband over the failure of a bank which he had started. So her devotion to prison reform was not motivated purely by Quaker spirituality, but also her dissatisfaction with it and, not least, her own personal ambition to be something more than the Quaker mother of eleven children.

Florence Nightingale, seeing she rejected all her very eligible suitors, was destined by Victorian custom to care for her rich parents. She rejected custom, however, and sought inspiration from the Lutheran deaconesses in Kaiserwerth in Germany.

Josephine Butler's husband was an Anglican clergyman, the headmaster of Liverpool College. The port of Liverpool was a popular centre for prostitution and there Josephine saw the problem in truly human terms. Prostitution was a symptom of the times because in 1871 there were in excess of three million unmarried adult women. It was the plight of women in Liverpool that induced Josephine Butler to become a crusader.[14]

These are stories we must celebrate in telling the story of laywomen. They illustrate the extraordinarily effective nurturing and pastoral role that women exercise. Yet we must note that these crusaders were subjected to vitriolic opposition. Eventually the Quakers recognised Elizabeth Fry as a minister so that she does not automatically fall into the category of a laywoman. We must be wary, therefore, in celebrating women's history, lest we think the battle is won for laywomen when ministerial recognition is given to particularly noted and gifted persons. Ordain women we must; but not so as to escape the 'equipping of all the saints' (Ephesians 4:12), not so as to neglect the recognition of all the gifts of the laity.

Some of the older historians like Williston Walker and Latourette have noted in their general histories that Christian churches gave increasing recognition to women. Latourette notes that in late medieval and Reformation times women were increasingly recognised for the contribution they were making to the church, and Latourette draws attention to their admission to the ordained ministry in Congregational and Baptist churches in the second half of the 19th century in both England and America.

Yet why the delay in the recognition of the rights of laywomen? The Age of Enlightenment and the evangelical revivals celebrated the autonomy of human reason and the validity of religious experience regardless of sex. In the 20th century, women won the right to vote and made a remarkable contribution to two world wars. We are forced to reflect why – as Hendrik Kraemer has written – the churches have been so retrograde concerning the role of laywomen.

Women in the Uniting Church

The women's movement of the 20th century is not content merely with books about women in medieval and Reformation times, nor with David Edward's 'Women as Crusaders'. They are necessary, though, to redress the imbalance in the telling of the church's story. A submission made by Australian women to the constitution commission of the proposed Uniting Church stated: 'For the true integration of women into the total ministry of the Church, positive steps will need to be taken to overcome the habits and stereotypes of centuries'.[15]

There could be no objection in principle to this because the *Basis of Union* acknowledges the gifts and graces of all members in the church, declaring that every gift has its corresponding service. Yet the debate revealed there was opposition as to the way in which the principles of the *Basis* were to be incorporated into the constitution and regulations. That a percentage of women members be required on councils and committees was opposed on the ground that to speak in figures was contrary to the spirit of Christianity. Dr Davis McCaughey then said that while in a sense it is true that a required percentage is contrary to the *Basis*, at certain historic moments in the church's life specific action needs to be taken in response to renewed understanding of the gospel. So it was agreed that for the first six years of the church's life, one third of the membership of councils should be women. In 1985, the N.S.W. Synod proposed in the national assembly that the one third principle be re-introduced. The motion was lost.[16]

It is cause for wonderment that this happened because it was too early to hope that Uniting Church members would be so enlightened as to make the one third principle unnecessary. Perhaps some members of the Assembly were influenced by the difficulty of not always being able to get the required representation of women. We are perhaps too close to the events themselves fully to understand the mood of the Assembly. There needs to be a deep searching of causes and effects, not least an understanding of Australian history and culture, to understand the issues more clearly. The story we have told reveals how much the cultural circumstances influence the way in which women's gifts are expressed and how difficult it is to break through institutional ways of understanding.

There is now a spate of fascinating literature, not least in Australia, that is addressing the role of women in history, so that increasingly we have the means to understand why progress has been slow. Psychology and sociology along with history are opening up new vistas of understanding. These are signs of hope that will make lay theology and the ministry of the whole people of God the vital agenda items for the church.

In the church made whole, there will be no silent voices because every voice will be heard in concert: a concert in praise of Christ in whom there is neither Jew nor Greek, bond nor free, male nor female.

Notes

1. Kraemer, p. 69. Reproduced by permission of The Lutterworth Press.
2. Witherington, p. 3. Reproduced by permission of Cambridge University Press.
3. Witherington, p. 3.
4. Witherington, p. 191.
5. Witherington, p. 198.
6. *Luther's Works*, vol. 51. p. 352.
7. Greaves, p. 26.
8. Whiting, p. 147.
9. Greaves, p. 79.
10. Greaves, p. 117.
11. Greaves, p. 133.
12. Rupp, p. 462.
13. Neill & Weber, p. 208.
14. Edwards, p. 289.
15. Franklin, pp. 124.
16. Franklin, p. 140.

4.
Making the church whole

A Turbulent, Seditious and Factious People is the title of Christopher Hill's 1989 prize winning book about John Bunyan and his church.[1] One has the feeling that for Bunyan such words were a sign of divine approval. They remind us that a church made whole is not necessarily a church at peace with society; nor, as Bunyan elsewhere notes, is it always in the best interests of the church that those within it are in perfect agreement with one another on all matters.

'It is very expedient that there should be heresies among us', Bunyan wrote provocatively in 1657, 'that thereby those which are indeed of the truth might be made manifest'.[2] That was not an admission that in the church anything goes; quite the contrary – in his Bedford congregation, members were very carefully chosen. It was not a case of believing as you like. It was the recognition that the people of God are always people on the way; the next battle, controversy or debate is never the last. The end of our pilgrim's progress lies with God, not with us. In Bonhoeffer's 'world come of age' theology, we could be forgiven for thinking we had already arrived. Bunyan is a good corrective to Bonhoeffer.[3]

I have begun with these references to Bunyan (whom his Anglican contemporaries probably thought of as a lay preacher) as a reminder that in depicting the laity as the forgotten factor in the church's story it would be wrong to think that all we have to do now is to redress the balance by asking the ordained ministers to engage in what has been called 'the skilful conduct of an orderly retreat'.[4]

The Canberra Assembly of the World Council of Churches has reminded us that the church is like a patchwork quilt in which many stories are pieced together to make a rich pattern. It is in the telling of those many stories and in stitching them together that the true pattern of the church's wholeness becomes visible. In the various patches we see how the various stories impinge one upon the other, contrast with one another, or supplement one another, in fact interpret one another. Without the rich, enduring texture of the story of the laity, however, the pattern of the whole is lopsided, lacking in colour and not designed to keep Christ's body healthy.

Still if the story of the church were only the story of the laity, the quilt would likewise be less than adequate. The story of the laity is crucial to the pattern of things; but without the stories also of apostles, prophets and martyrs, bishops, priests and deacons, monks and nuns, ministers and missionaries, churches and cathedrals, congregations and denominations, even assemblies, synods and boards, the quilt would be no good.

We can highlight the story of the laity by concentrating on some of the major strands in the rich tapestry of the church's life. They are ministry, mission, ecumenism and theology. In seeking to make these stories relevant to Australia, the Uniting Church came into being. It is a stroke of genius that we call ourselves Uniting, rather than United. We have not yet arrived; we are people on the way to the promised end.

In ministry

Jesus Christ is the essential minister in the church, so it is Christ's ministry the church seeks to proclaim and make relevant to the world. In the early church those with particular responsibility – bishops and ministers – saw their ministry as calling those whom God calls. When the Roman Empire recognised Christianity, it was almost inevitable that the ministers should become authoritative in character. They came to be seen not only as calling the people to their vocation in Christ, but as ensuring that the people duly participated in their civic duties. The church was organised according to the necessities of civic administration. Roman institutionalism tended to replace Christian fellowship; worship in formal basilicas tended to replace gatherings in Christian homes. Christendom had begun bringing gifts and graces; but also bringing new challenges to the essential ministry of Christ.

The real dogfight at the Reformation was about ministry. Certainly Luther saw it as the failure of the church to proclaim to the laity, plagued as he was with deep anxiety. The cheap grace offered by the purchase of a letter of full forgiveness made nonsense of the confessional, giving little assurance of the costly grace of the ministry of Christ. Indulgences were undoubtedly popular; but in the 16th century a more deeply satisfying discipline of the soul was needed. Appalled at papal policy and ineptitude, Luther nailed up his theses and within a few years was proclaiming the priesthood of all believers.

That was a liberating word for anxious souls and would-be reformers. It was a giant step forward in making the church whole. In the circumstances, however, a subtle and important change took place in the ordained ministry. It came to see itself, not as calling the people God calls, but as calling the church to be what it was meant to be. Unable to divest itself of the Christendom heritage, Protestantism gave way to national churches, the Lutheran, the Church of Scotland, the Church of England, whose ministers believed they were obliged to proclaim the virtues of reform and the evils of popery.

One cannot help but be impressed reading the Protestant literature of the 16th and 17th centuries how much polemic purports to pass for ministry. Though not a national church, even Congregationalists thrived on a polemical spirituality. In a quaint phrase the early Congregationalists declared the Church of England to be 'but halfly reformed'. All our Protestant ancestors enjoyed hurling polemic against the Pope.

To reassert the essential ministry of Jesus Christ, the early monks and nuns retreated into poverty. To recover the ministry of Jesus Christ from the corruptions of the 16th century, the reformers resorted to lay politics, Luther appealed to the princes, Calvin to the Town Council. All baptised Christians are kings and priests before God and therefore have a responsibility before God to use political means to reform Christian society.

It has been argued that the Evangelical Revival and the rise of Methodism saved England from violent revolution such as occurred in France, that the development of trades unions owes much to the sense of human dignity that evangelical preaching inspired.[5] There is considerable evidence to support this conclusion and after all we should not be surprised that the preaching of the availability of free grace for every sinful soul should serve to remind humble people of their dignity and worth before God and their rights before the nation. Local preachers, far more numerous than itinerant preachers, pursuing their everyday work, immersed in day-to-day conflicts and face-to-face relationships, were inevitably 'in the world'. They were seeking an all-embracing fabric of meaning to make sense of their world.

We would fail in our understanding of history, however, if we did not also observe, as a recent historian has done speaking of Primitive Methodists in the English Midlands, that when set in their own words, the belief of local preachers does not readily transfer into political terms.[6] Dutiful local preachers believed politics to be a diversion from the real work of conversion. Even if we admit that the gospel they preached had ramifications they could not readily appreciate, we can begin to see that the tension between faith and politics, so real in the Uniting Church, is obviously not a new phenomenon. Evangelicalism paradoxically inspired both a new sense of responsibility for the world and an emphasis on a spiritual message that saw worldly politics as a snare and delusion.

In mission

Another of the major threads in the tapestry of the church's life is mission. The early church was a missionary church.

When Christianity was institutionalised within the Roman Empire, it did not cease to be missionary. The attraction of Roman civilisation to the barbarian hordes meant that they were also attracted to Christianity. Converts were not always orthodox in belief and indeed many pagan practices persisted and needed to be baptised, so to speak, into Christianity. Itinerant monks carried out the work of mission and the monasteries themselves became the centres of instruction.

At the time of the Reformation, Western Europe was considered to be Christian. It would not have occurred to a member of society in the 16th century to be an atheist. There was a sense then in which the church at the end of the 15th century had ceased to be missionary. It was not surprising that Luther and Calvin should be relatively unconcerned with what we call mission.

The age of pietism in the 18th century and the evangelical revival recalled the church to its original missionary responsibility. Fascinatingly it called the church to be 'whole at heart'. It saw ministry as calling the world to Christ. In the face of moribund institutionalism, evangelicals made their appeal to the heart, not with a view to downgrading human reason, but rather to assert the appeal of Christianity to the whole human personality.

This emphasis on personal faith promised to make denominations and classes relative, to recall the church to the missionary task and assert the apostolate of the laity. Just as early Protestantism's doctrine of justifying faith put an end to the difference in status between the laity and the monastic orders, so now the evangelical experience promised to be the unifying factor, replacing the old institutional unity of Christendom and the enforced unity of state religion.

In the context of the Uniting Church, Methodism has been the inheritor and exponent of this tradition. It has emphasised the role of the laity. We recalled earlier that Stephen Neill has written that English Methodism was the greatest organisation for the employment of lay forces that has ever existed. Indeed the horizon of the Christian enterprise became 'the world'. The world is my parish, Wesley said. In effect that meant the laity could not be 'cribbed, cabined and confined' within the old parish structures nor forced to submit meekly to clerical authority. There is a sense in which the laity came of age at the time of the evangelical revival. Another giant step forward in restoring the role of the laity had been taken.

The colonial origins of churches in Australia owe a good deal to this sense of world mission. The first chaplains were evangelicals. The first Congregational Church in New South

Wales was planted by lay agents of the London Missionary Society. These were people sensing a liberation from old ideas of Christendom.[7] It was not only the allurements of lands hitherto unknown geographically; but of a new world situation historically that inspired their sense of adventure. The world had become a mission field in which the gifts of all the people of God were necessary. Perhaps poverty at home had a hand in making the layman, William Carey, the first missionary to India; yet his pleasing dream of an ecumenical missionary enterprise was indicative of this new sense of a world called to participate in Christ.

In medieval times it was thought that the best way for a lay person to be truly religious was to become a monk or a nun, remembering, of course, that the monastic calling was originally a lay calling. Protestantism changed that. Daily work in the world, Luther declared, was just as holy a calling as that of life in the monastery. The evangelical revival underlined the place of the world as the sphere of saving Christian experience. It therefore exemplified the role of the laity in the Christian mission. It opened up the possibility of industry and overseas commerce as spheres of missionary activity and lay ministry. It questioned the effectiveness of local parish organisation and experimented with the meeting, the congregation, and the voluntary society. It began to show us how the diversity of lay gifts and vocations participates in the mission of God.

Its success is our problem. We think we can repeat the techniques of the 19th century in the very different world of the 20th century. When we look at the history of the church, context is always crucial. We can understand why the church adopted the organisation of the Roman Empire; we can understand why, despite the contrary desire of the reformers, denominations came into being. The historical circumstances of the 20th century in which the church is called to participate in the mission of God mean that we must ask whether past responses are adequate. New occasions teach new duties. We have to discern the universal significance of Christ in a world where respect for other faiths is paramount: where dialogue must replace the old desire to convert.

Quite rightly the Uniting Church in Australia has declared that the mission and renewal of the church in Australia, its being made whole, does not depend on perpetuating denominational divisions because, however valid at the time, they were forged in a different place at a different time. Excited by them we discern their historical relevance and celebrate them in a new context. We remember gratefully; but we dare not try to repeat the past. That would be to deny the pilgrimage we are now called to make along the path of multiculturalism.

In ecumenism

That brings us to another of the stories that contribute to the church's wholeness. The ecumenical strand is one that has always helped to bring clarity to the pattern of the church's life, though not until the 20th century with the formation of the World Council of Churches has it won the attention it deserves. This is a story that the Uniting Church has a special responsibility to tell because its inauguration was an act of courageous ecumenism, one of the most significant events in Australian religious history.

It has been said that the laity is naturally ecumenical. They do not work in Methodist labour unions or Congregational stores or live in Presbyterian streets, let alone Uniting Church country clubs. Many remarkable ecumenical lay initiatives throughout history have been taken by laymen and women. John D. Rockefeller Jr said in 1916 that he would not give any more money to denominational institutions because he favoured religious co-operation as the way to bring the kingdom of God on earth.[8] We know now that more than philanthropy is needed. But that must not blind us to the ecumenical significance of lay witness expressed in philanthropy. Philanthropy, as distinct from charity which is bound to the past, has been defined as open to the future. Charity begins at home, but philanthropy, largely because of its munificence, is freed from such restraints.

One of the great ecumenical pioneers was a layman, John R. Mott. He conceived of his mission as calling the world to Christ: the evangelisation of the world in his generation. It was an extraordinarily inspired attempt to enter fully into the church's wholeness. In its origins, it owed much to the evangelical revival's conviction that by its very nature the Christian experience of salvation must be shared. In a real sense the ecumenical movement began with the modern missionary movement, with William Carey's 'pleasing dream'.

In 1948, the missionary movement, the life and work movement and the faith and order movement came together to form the World Council of Churches. It was a demonstration of the wholeness of the church in the framework of world history. Two world wars had demonstrated that the old Roman idea of Christendom was disintegrating.⁹ Pursuing that vision, it is highly significant that it was the ecumenical movement that initiated the new awareness of the role of the laity in the late 1950s and early 60s. And it was to be expected that the World Council would encourage enquiry into the status of women in the church. That also was germane to its understanding of wholeness.

Some are now disenchanted with the ecumenical vision. It seems so obvious, given the theology of reconciliation and the nature of the unity we are given and must seek in Christ, that we should be well on the way to a renewed wholeness, whereas what has been revealed is just how difficult it all is. The Uniting Church from the grass roots up is painfully aware of the cost of uniting. Yet should we have expected otherwise? There is a cross at the heart of the church's wholeness. The form which ecumenism has taken is conciliar. By their very nature, councils must deal with conflict and seek resolution. The more representative a council is, the more problems and conflicts it must entertain. The more councils seek to be relevant to the whole inhabited earth, the more they will be caught in the political tensions of our time. Was not the cross of Jesus a tragic symbol of the tension between Roman might and Jewish nationalism?

In theology

Theology is perhaps the most exciting, subtle and intellectually demanding way of telling the Christian story. When, in the light of scripture and the Christian tradition, we try to see how, for example, the stories of ministry, mission and ecumenism relate to one another, we are in the area of theology. Theology is faith seeking a pattern of understanding. Doing theology is about where lay people are: sharing their fears, their pains, their frustrations, and struggling to interpret the will of God into social realities. To do this we need not only the witness of the

Bible and tradition, we must also understand the powers that run the world and learn the languages of the community.

The Christian story does not make satisfying sense without theology. It is properly the work of the whole people of God to tell this story. It is not reserved for the clergy or the professional theologians alone. One of the blessings that liberation theologies have brought us is that they emphasise that theology is the work of the people. Christian theology cannot really be anything else but an articulation of how the ministry of Christ becomes the ministry of all the people.

The 20th century shows that the laity is increasingly able to bring enormous intellectual resources to bear on the complex issues that are now woven into the story. One of the mistakes of the past was that the ministry of the laity was seen as the ministry of heart and hand, while the ministry of the mind belonged to the ordained ministers. Without that contribution of the mind of the laity, the whole story cannot be told and Christian witness is truncated. Of course theology demands intellectual gifts as any artful storyteller demonstrates; but of such gifts the clergy do not have a monopoly. And such, for example, are the global and ethical issues confronting us that the intellectual gifts of the laity are essential for the theological enterprise. It is not a time for one-dimensional thinking.

Indeed since the 1970s a revolution has been taking place in theology. It is the recognition that faith seeking understanding involves not the mind only but the whole person.

In the past, theology was very dispassionate; we now believe that our emotions and passions must not be excluded from knowing God. It is with the intellect plus the other faculties of the human being that we need to do theology. It is loving God with all our heart, mind, soul and strength which is the proper stuff of theology. So it would be very strange if, in the desire to give meaning to the fabric of life, only the clergy were to do theology, because they cannot know all the passions that excite human beings. It would be equally strange if only men did theology. The men and women of the laity are not beneficiaries of theology; they are its participants.

The Uniting Church committed itself in the *Basis of Union* to a full recognition of the gifts of the laity; not only as a matter of pastoral concern, but also as a matter of theological integrity. Our laywomen are helping us to see that no one group can be whole at the expense of another. Despite the accusation that the Uniting Church is strong on pastoral care and weak on doctrine (a not altogether fair criticism because there is just a hint in it that theology can be separated off from people) we know nowadays that good pastoral care demands good theology.

Throughout the history of the church, as we have seen, there has been a tendency either to clericalise the laity or laicise the clergy. One of the strengths of the *Basis of Union* is its inherent conviction that this trap must always be avoided without, as it were, homogeonising ministers and people into a bland mixture. God, it is true, has never left his church without especially calling some to minister the Word and the sacraments. Without the Word and the sacraments the church cannot live. Yet the *Basis* also declares that these are not the only gifts of ministry. All the diverse gifts of the Spirit have their corresponding service. Thus when the doctrines of the priesthood of all believers and the doctrine of spiritual gifts are correlated, we are well on the way to accepting with joy all the gifts of the whole people of God.

A turning wheel that causes no motion elsewhere does not belong to a machine. At the local level, we are still struggling to get all the wheels of a united and uniting laity to become a well-oiled machine. We need to tell our theology story better on the question of authority: to make a renewed understanding of the laity a significant factor on that agenda. A good beginning was made at the Uniting Church conference, *The Church Made Whole*, in January 1990. I want to oil the wheel of authority in just two particular ways.

The first concerns spiritual leadership at the parish level. Mature ministers are happy to let the laity exercise their gifts and exercise the authority appropriate to those gifts as long as they are checked and balanced by the corporate life of the parish or the congregation. Laity unused to such a scenario sometimes find it daunting. It does not seem right, for example, for a church meeting to make a decision unless an ordained person is in the chair. On the other hand, one has to admit that sometimes we ordained ministers try to hold on to authority and power to cover our own unwillingness to endure the more democratic process or to hide our own personal weaknesses and superficial spiritual understanding. Most are very hardworking, self-giving and imbued with marvellous common sense. Yet we dare not hide our clerical heads in the sand about a matter of supreme importance in making the church whole.

There is a heart-rending scene in 'Shadowlands', the play about the life of C. S. Lewis, where Lewis wants his old clergyman friend to marry him to his dear friend, Joy, a divorced woman, who is actually dying of cancer. His friend refuses to marry a divorced person. 'I do not make the rules', he says. In a delicate pastoral situation like that, simple recourse to arbitrary rules tears sacred human relationships apart. Christian authority is more than a matter of rules. It is a matter of theological discernment and deep sensitivity to the gospel of grace on the part of ministers and laity doing theology together in the context of everyday life.

The parishes of the UCA do require leadership that is more than an application of rules. All that we have said about spiritual gifts and the essential place of the laity do not cancel out the gifts of leadership. To be the representative of the Word and the sacraments to a fellowship of people makes that leadership a necessity. Yet it is a very special kind of leadership or presidency; it is a community leadership style that fosters the laity's gifts. It becomes wellnigh an impossible calling unless there is an adequate theological understanding of where authority lies and how Christ's will is made known.

Theologians and lay people skilled in management need to talk together about the subtle distinction the gospel draws between ministerial (or persuasive) and magisterial (or coercive) authority. They need to discuss together how the church must always try to give expression to Christlike authority. Though I would not be surprised if the best management techniques are not sometimes more loving than church techniques. Still, in other respects, management techniques may be so ruthless they deny the gospel.

The second authority issue relates to the proper use of the experience of the laity in the world. We have not taken the apostolate of the laity fully seriously merely by having them read lessons, do prayers and preach sermons, though such ministries are a helpful sign and use of lay gifts. The three basic channels of authority that have been manifested in church history are (a) the church itself, its hierarchy and tradition; (b) the Bible; and (c) the immediate guidance of the Holy Spirit in individual experience. According to recent research the majority of Christian laity in Australia place a priority on religious subjectivity and personal experience.[10]

Protestant evangelicalism may be said to have asserted the importance of the 'heart' in matters of faith; but at its best it knew that personal religion must always be rooted and grounded in the biblical witness and illumined by the light of tradition. Given the new understanding of theology that we noted earlier, we may not assert an arbitrary priority of scripture and tradition over against personal experience. We must abandon any suspicion of ordinary people's often inarticulate experience of God and begin informing it with the vast experience of the Bible and the Christian tradition. Then we can begin to articulate a theology of the whole people of God that is alive and relevant for today.

A church, however, which has responded to the subjectivity of the age and is merely a source of peace and refuge to troubled hearts is missing out on the challenge the 20th century poses for justice, peace and the integrity of creation. A church that sentimentalises the story of the cross is not really responding to the deep pain and suffering of our time. A church which will not bring the gifts of heart and mind and soul to the preaching of the gospel is in no position to call for peace, to relate to people of other faiths, to win the 'greenies' to a Christian doctrine of creation, nor stem the tide of secularism.

Making the church whole is not a matter of being in perfect agreement; it is not a matter of passive acceptance of prevailing politics; no, it is a matter of all God's people being on the way together to the celestial city. It becomes a vital and inspiring pilgrimage when we love God and one another with all our heart, mind, soul and strength.

Let me change the image. Stereo recordings called 'Music Minus One' give amateur musicians the chance to enter the realm of the professional orchestra by playing the part that has been left out. There is no 'music' without that part. We all need to find our part without which the symphony of life in the church would be unmusical. When the laity and its needs are no longer the forgotten factor, we can all make music in full harmony.

Notes
1. See Ezra 4:12-16.
2. Hill, p. 91.
3. Paul, p. 64.
4. Moltmann, p. 46.
5. See R. F. Wearmouth, *Methodism and the Working Class Movements of England*, 1937.
6. Sheils & Wood, p. 346.
7. Moltmann, p. 10.
8. Butt & Wright, p. 127.
9. Moltmann, p. 8.
10. P. Hughes, *The Australian Clergy*.

Bibliography

Yves M. J. Congar, (tr. D. Attwater), *Lay People in the Church*, rev. ed., Geoffrey Chapman, London, 1985.

Roland Bainton, *Women of the Reformation*, 3 vols, Augsburg Publishing House, Minneapolis, 1971, 1973 & 1977.

H. Butt with E. Wright (eds), *At the Edge of Hope: Christian Laity in Paradox*, Seabury Press, New York, 1978.

Louis Bouyer, *A History of Christian Spirituality, vol. 1: The Spirituality of the New Testament and the Fathers*, Burns & Oates, London, 1963.

Calvin, *Institutes*, ed. J. T. McNeill, tr. F. L.. Battles, Westminster Press, Philadelphia, 1960.

George Davies & Gordon Rupp, *A History of the Methodist Church in Great Britain, vol., 2*, Epworth Press, 1978.

Leonard Doohan, *The Lay-Centered Church*, Winston Press, Minneapolis, 1984.

David Edwards, *Christian England, vol. 3*, William Collins, London, 1984.

Elizabeth Schussler Fiorenza, *In Memory of Her*, Crossroad, New York, 1983.

Margaret Ann Franklin, ed., *The Force of the Feminine*, Allen & Unwin, Sydney, 1986.

Mark Gibbs & T. Ralph Morton, *God's Frozen People*, Westminster Press, Philadelphia, 1965.

— —- *God's Lively People*, Westminster Press, Philadelphia, 1971.

R. L. Greaves, *Triumph Over Silence*, Greenwood Press, Westport, 1985.

Christopher Hill, *A Turbulent, Seditious and Factious People*, 1989, Oxford University Press, 1989.

Philip Hughes, *The Australian Clergy*, Christian Research Association, Melbourne, 1989.

Hendrik Kraemer, *A Theology of the Laity*, Lutterworth Press, London, 1958.

Kenneth Kirk, ed., *The Apostolic Ministry*, Hodder & Stoughton, London, 1946.

Luther's Works, *Sermons 1*, Muhlenberg Press, Philadelphia, 1959.

John Macquarrie, *The Faith of the People of God*, S.C.M. Press, London, 1972.

T. W. Manson, *Ministry and Priesthood: Christ's and Ours*, Epworth Press, London, 1958.

Jurgen Moltmann, *The Church in the Power of the Spirit*, S.C.M. Press, London, 1977.

Stephen Neill & Hans-Ruedi Weber, *The Layman in Christian History*, S.C.M. Press, London, 1963.

T. E. O'Connell, ed., *Vatican II and its Documents*, Michael Glazier, Wilmington, Delaware, 1986

Elaine Pagels, *The Gnostic Gospels*, Random House, New York, 1979.

Albert Peel & Leland Carlson, *The Writings of Robert Harrison and Robert Browne*, Allen and Unwin, London, 1953.

Robert S. Paul, *Freedom with Order*, United Church Press, New York, 1987.

— —- *An Apologeticall Narration*, United Church Press, New York, 1963

Gordon Rupp, *Religion in England*, 1688-1791, Clarendon Press, Oxford, 1986.

Paul A. Russell, *Lay Theology in the Reformation*, Cambridge University Press, 1986.

Edward Schillebeeckx, *The Church with a Human Face*, S.C.M. Press, London, 1985.

W. J. Sheils & Diana Wood, eds., *The Ministry: Clerical and Lay*, (Studies in Church History, 26), Basil Blackwell, Oxford, 1989.

R. F. Wearmouth, *Methodism and the Working Class Movements of England*, 2nd ed., Epworth Press, London, 1947.

Robert Whiting, *The Blind Devotion of the People*, Cambridge University Press, 1989.

Ben Witherington III, *Women in the Earliest Churches*, Cambridge University Press, 1988.